How To Solve ALL IT Problems!

Written By Terry Billitch
Cover photograph by Elnur Amikishiyev
Copyright Argle Bargle Publishing Ltd

Foreword and Disclaimer.

This book is a novelty joke book and not intended as a serious problem solving guide, we suggest using it as a notepad.

The Author and Publisher take no responsibility for any advice contained within the book. This book is purely for entertainment purposes only and should not be viewed as a genuine way of solving IT issues.

No computers were harmed during the making of this book.

Second Edition

**How to solve 95% of all IT Problems-
Turn it off and then back on again!**

**Copyright Argle Bargle Publishing Ltd
www.argle-bargle.co.uk**

How to solve 95% of all IT Problems- Turn it off and then back on again!

**Copyright Argle Bargle Publishing Ltd
www.argle-bargle.co.uk**

**How to solve 95% of all IT Problems-
Turn it off and then back on again!**

**Copyright Argle Bargle Publishing Ltd
www.argle-bargle.co.uk**

How to solve 95% of all IT Problems- Turn it off and then back on again!

Copyright Argle Bargle Publishing Ltd
www.argle-bargle.co.uk

How to solve 95% of all IT Problems-
Turn it off and then back on again!

Copyright Argle Bargle Publishing Ltd
www.argle-bargle.co.uk

How to solve 95% of all IT Problems- Turn it off and then back on again!

Copyright Argle Bargle Publishing Ltd
www.argle-bargle.co.uk

**How to solve 95% of all IT Problems-
Turn it off and then back on again!**

**Copyright Argle Bargle Publishing Ltd
www.argle-bargle.co.uk**

**How to solve 95% of all IT Problems-
Turn it off and then back on again!**

Copyright Argle Bargle Publishing Ltd
www.argle-bargle.co.uk

How to solve 95% of all IT Problems- Turn it off and then back on again!

Copyright Argle Bargle Publishing Ltd
www.argle-bargle.co.uk

How to solve 95% of all IT Problems- Turn it off and then back on again!

Copyright Argle Bargle Publishing Ltd
www.argle-bargle.co.uk

**How to solve 95% of all IT Problems-
Turn it off and then back on again!**

**Copyright Argle Bargle Publishing Ltd
www.argle-bargle.co.uk**

**How to solve 95% of all IT Problems-
Turn it off and then back on again!**

**Copyright Argle Bargle Publishing Ltd
www.argle-bargle.co.uk**

**How to solve 95% of all IT Problems-
Turn it off and then back on again!**

Copyright Argle Bargle Publishing Ltd
www.argle-bargle.co.uk

How to solve 95% of all IT Problems- Turn it off and then back on again!

**Copyright Argle Bargle Publishing Ltd
www.argle-bargle.co.uk**

**How to solve 95% of all IT Problems-
Turn it off and then back on again!**

**Copyright Argle Bargle Publishing Ltd
www.argle-bargle.co.uk**

How to solve 95% of all IT Problems- Turn it off and then back on again!

Copyright Argle Bargle Publishing Ltd
www.argle-bargle.co.uk

**How to solve 95% of all IT Problems-
Turn it off and then back on again!**

**Copyright Argle Bargle Publishing Ltd
www.argle-bargle.co.uk**

**How to solve 95% of all IT Problems-
Turn it off and then back on again!**

**Copyright Argle Bargle Publishing Ltd
www.argle-bargle.co.uk**

**How to solve 95% of all IT Problems-
Turn it off and then back on again!**

**Copyright Argle Bargle Publishing Ltd
www.argle-bargle.co.uk**

**How to solve 95% of all IT Problems-
Turn it off and then back on again!**

Copyright Argle Bargle Publishing Ltd
www.argle-bargle.co.uk

How to solve 95% of all IT Problems- Turn it off and then back on again!

Copyright Argle Bargle Publishing Ltd
www.argle-bargle.co.uk

**How to solve 95% of all IT Problems-
Turn it off and then back on again!**

**Copyright Argle Bargle Publishing Ltd
www.argle-bargle.co.uk**

**How to solve 95% of all IT Problems-
Turn it off and then back on again!**

**Copyright Argle Bargle Publishing Ltd
www.argle-bargle.co.uk**

**How to solve 95% of all IT Problems-
Turn it off and then back on again!**

**Copyright Argle Bargle Publishing Ltd
www.argle-bargle.co.uk**

**How to solve 95% of all IT Problems-
Turn it off and then back on again!**

Copyright Argle Bargle Publishing Ltd
www.argle-bargle.co.uk

**How to solve 95% of all IT Problems-
Turn it off and then back on again!**

**Copyright Argle Bargle Publishing Ltd
www.argle-bargle.co.uk**

How to solve 95% of all IT Problems- Turn it off and then back on again!

Copyright Argle Bargle Publishing Ltd
www.argle-bargle.co.uk

**How to solve 95% of all IT Problems-
Turn it off and then back on again!**

**Copyright Argle Bargle Publishing Ltd
www.argle-bargle.co.uk**

How to solve 95% of all IT Problems- Turn it off and then back on again!

**Copyright Argle Bargle Publishing Ltd
www.argle-bargle.co.uk**

**How to solve 95% of all IT Problems-
Turn it off and then back on again!**

**Copyright Argle Bargle Publishing Ltd
www.argle-bargle.co.uk**

How to solve 95% of all IT Problems- Turn it off and then back on again!

Copyright Argle Bargle Publishing Ltd
www.argle-bargle.co.uk

**How to solve 95% of all IT Problems-
Turn it off and then back on again!**

**Copyright Argle Bargle Publishing Ltd
www.argle-bargle.co.uk**

**How to solve 95% of all IT Problems-
Turn it off and then back on again!**

**Copyright Argle Bargle Publishing Ltd
www.argle-bargle.co.uk**

**How to solve 95% of all IT Problems-
Turn it off and then back on again!**

**Copyright Argle Bargle Publishing Ltd
www.argle-bargle.co.uk**

**How to solve 95% of all IT Problems-
Turn it off and then back on again!**

**Copyright Argle Bargle Publishing Ltd
www.argle-bargle.co.uk**

How to solve 95% of all IT Problems- Turn it off and then back on again!

Copyright Argle Bargle Publishing Ltd
www.argle-bargle.co.uk

**How to solve 95% of all IT Problems-
Turn it off and then back on again!**

**Copyright Argle Bargle Publishing Ltd
www.argle-bargle.co.uk**

**How to solve 95% of all IT Problems-
Turn it off and then back on again!**

**Copyright Argle Bargle Publishing Ltd
www.argle-bargle.co.uk**

How to solve 95% of all IT Problems-
Turn it off and then back on again!

Copyright Argle Bargle Publishing Ltd
www.argle-bargle.co.uk

**How to solve 95% of all IT Problems-
Turn it off and then back on again!**

**Copyright Argle Bargle Publishing Ltd
www.argle-bargle.co.uk**

**How to solve 95% of all IT Problems-
Turn it off and then back on again!**

**Copyright Argle Bargle Publishing Ltd
www.argle-bargle.co.uk**

**How to solve 95% of all IT Problems-
Turn it off and then back on again!**

**Copyright Argle Bargle Publishing Ltd
www.argle-bargle.co.uk**

How to solve 95% of all IT Problems- Turn it off and then back on again!

Copyright Argle Bargle Publishing Ltd
www.argle-bargle.co.uk

**How to solve 95% of all IT Problems-
Turn it off and then back on again!**

Copyright Argle Bargle Publishing Ltd
www.argle-bargle.co.uk

How to solve 95% of all IT Problems- Turn it off and then back on again!

Copyright Argle Bargle Publishing Ltd
www.argle-bargle.co.uk

**How to solve 95% of all IT Problems-
Turn it off and then back on again!**

**Copyright Argle Bargle Publishing Ltd
www.argle-bargle.co.uk**

**How to solve 95% of all IT Problems-
Turn it off and then back on again!**

**Copyright Argle Bargle Publishing Ltd
www.argle-bargle.co.uk**

Printed in Great Britain
by Amazon